SUCCESS SECRETS

STEPH ADAMS

SUCCESS SECRETS

*Success Secrets features a powerful
selection of inspirational advice on how to overcome
failure and achieve success.*

*From men and women entrepreneurs around the world,
giving you key pieces of advice so that you can be
encouraged and empowered in achieving your goals.*

SUCCESS SECRETS

Copyright @ 2021 Steph Adams

All rights reserved.

Design and published by Steph Adams

No part of this book may be used or produced in any manner whatsoever without written permission, except in the case of brief quotations embodied in critical articles and reviews.

FROM THE AUTHOR

From a young age I was introduced to various people from all walks of life. My Grandfather Phillip Rennel Adams was a Q.C who brought the drinking age down from 21 to 18 in Australia. He had a very strong work ethic and has inspired me through out my life.

Some of the best conversations you can have, are when people really open up to you from the heart. I still remember a conversation in my early teens with an old aboriginal man up in Broome. My father had taken me up there on business and I remember this kind man speaking about his life growing up and the love he had of the land.

'Success Secrets' is a compilation of inspiring advice from successful entrepreneurs. Advice that is shared even through victory and defeat.

After spending the last two decades in the publishing industry and interviewing great men and women around the world, I wanted to shortlist the most powerful pieces of advice I have been given.

On the following pages are success secrets that have been told to me as well as some sourced and never before published.

I hope you enjoy and keep striving toward your dreams.

Steph Adams

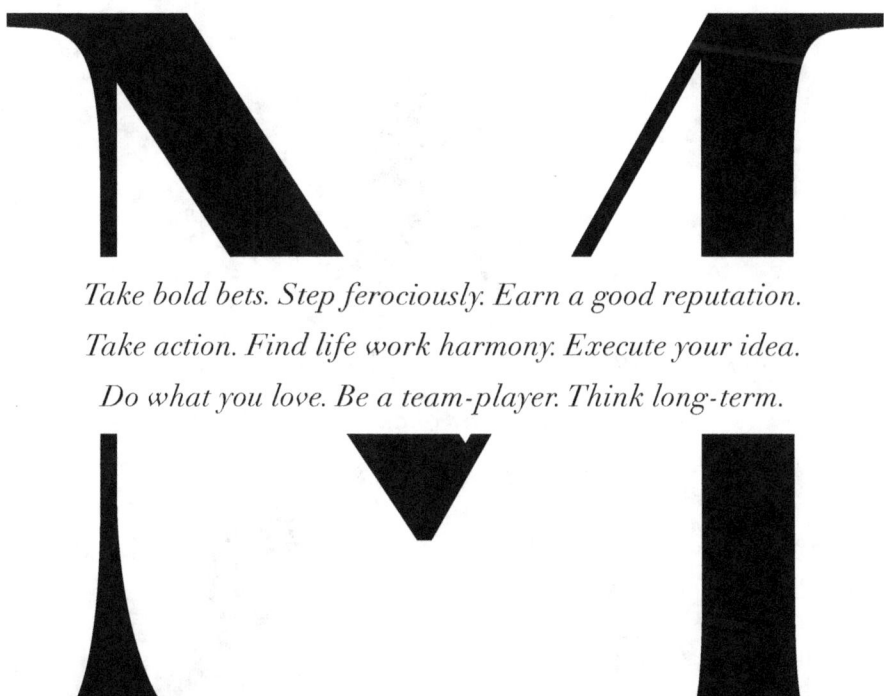

Take bold bets. Step ferociously. Earn a good reputation. Take action. Find life work harmony. Execute your idea. Do what you love. Be a team-player. Think long-term.

JEFF BEZOS

*Appreciate all the baby steps it takes to take a leap forward.
Write, collect images and make mood boards.
Find co-dreamers; people who support your dreams.*

ELLE MACPHERSON

*We're here to put a dent in the universe.
Otherwise why else even be here?
Sometimes life is going to hit you in the head
with a brick. Don't lose faith.*

STEVE JOBS

You have to feel confident. If you don't, then you are going to be hesitant and defensive, and there'll be a lot of things working against you. You have to take things into your own hands. Fate pulls you in different directions.

CLINT EASTWOOD

We are all wired differently. We are all unique and special.
Realize you develop superpowers by misfiring and mistakes.

SCOTT STEINDORFF

American Film Producer

Surround yourself with people who challenge you, teach you, and push you to be your best self.

BILL GATES

*The key to realizing a dream is to focus
not on success but significance, and then
even the small steps and little victories along
your path will take on greater meaning*

OPRAH

E

*Experiment and take risks.
Remember to look beyond your own personal passions
and be part of something larger than yourself.*

ARIANNA HUFFINGTON

My thoughts before a big race are usually pretty simple. I tell myself: Get out of the blocks, run your race, stay relaxed. If you run and race you will win... Channel your energy. Focus.

CARL LEWIS
Track and field star athlete

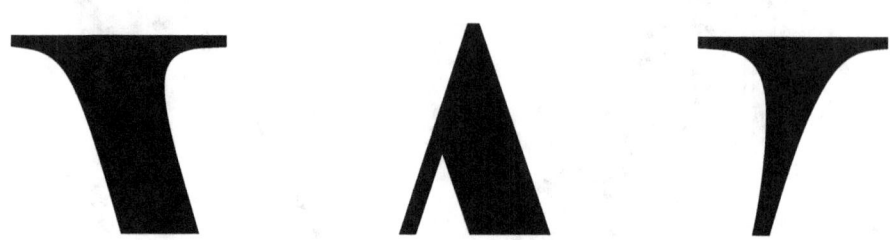

We must use time creatively, in the knowledge that the time is always ripe to do the right thing.

MARTIN LUTHER KING JR

Do not feel entitled! Success doesn't just happen to you. You can be successful and kind. You don't have to step on people to get where you need to be.

RACHEL ZOE

Stay curious.
Everything can be beautiful if you take your time.
Follow your dreams.

AERIN LAUDER

*Don't be scared by social media.
But don't be controlled by it either.
Be the person you hope your daughter looks up to.*

INDIA HICKS

B

*Be committed and consistent.
Determination is key.
Stay focused on your project and protective of it's integrity.*

MONIQUE LHUILLIER

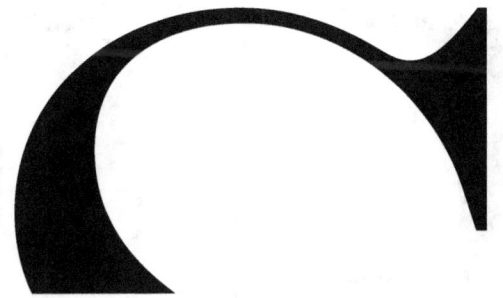

Success begins at that magical moment when you declare to yourself, your friends and the universe that you believe you can do something different.

NATALIE MASSENET

Have the passion of a storyteller, the resilience of an entreprenuer and the creativity of an artist. When you fall down and fail, pick yourself back up and start walking toward your goal.

JO MALONE

K

Keep constantly evolving and doing things differently.

JEFF LEATHAM

*Find your voice and be consistent with it.
Always engage with your audience.*

ELLA MILLS

*Trust your instincts, back your judgement,
and don't let anyone define you.*

JULIE BISHOP

Let your hard work speak for itself. Always be pulled together as it sets your mind to be productive.

OLIVIA PALERMO

We have to reshape our own perception of how we view ourselves. We have to step up as women and take the lead.

BEYONCE

*Don't do anything just for money, do it
for your passion and money will come later.*

MELISSA ODABASH

*Only those who risk going too far
can possibly find out how far one can go.*

T. S ELIOT

Trust yourself, stay true to your own vision, but also be willing to take a step back and look at the bigger picture.

SOPHIA WEBSTER

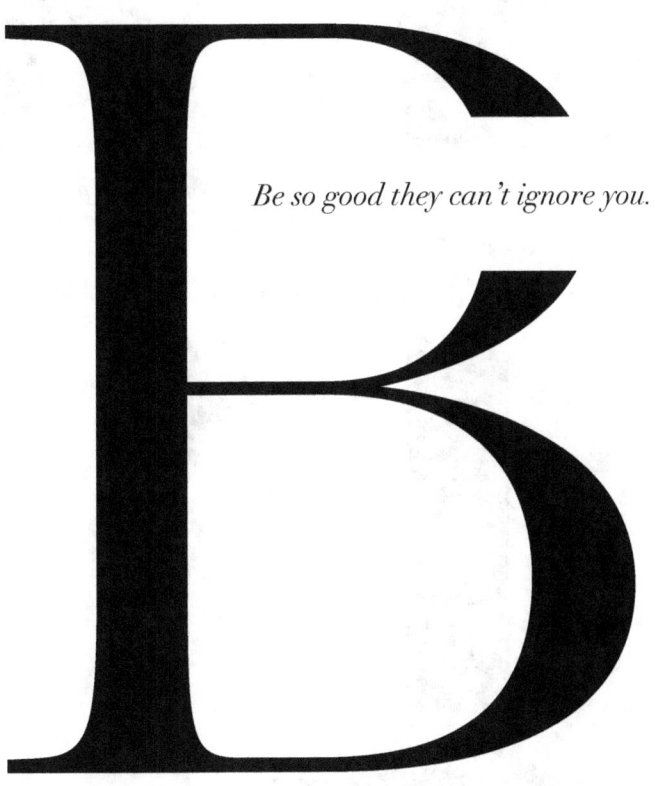

Be so good they can't ignore you.

STEVE MARTIN

Focus on what you should be doing and not on what everyone else is doing. Reinvest your sales back into your business.

JENNIFER FISHER

Knowing that nothing worthwhile was built overnight - you will be challenged, you will be questioned and you will be misunderstood. Push through because it's usually the hardest of times that you see progress.

LORNA JANE

Fill a void in your field.
All experience is good experience.
Work for people you admire and never give up.

LEESA EVANS

It's important to adapt a marketing strategy to your target group, thus social media is definitely a key aspect in strategy.

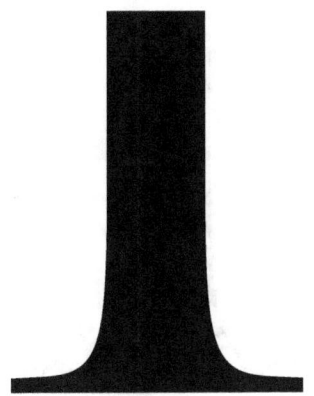

NEGIN MIRSALEHI

VI

You need a unique idea, you need to be passionate about your craft and you have to work hard.

BOBBI BROWN

*Never give up on your dream.
Write down a plan and strategy to make that
dream happen and start on it today.*

MEGAN HESS

*Things don't just fall into your lap.
You have to work hard to get where you want to be.
Use failure as your inspiration and build on that.
Build a network of people who you trust.*

STEPH ADAMS

Rejection is an inevitable part of the journey to success.

CAMILLA CLEESE

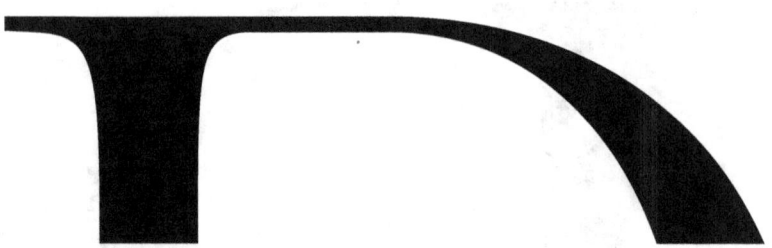

Success is 100% about execution. You can have the best ideas in the world, but without execution they remain in the abyss. Research everything you can about how others have done it before you and make sure your mindset remains positive and open to all possibilities. That's when anything is truly possible.

SAMANTHA BRETT

Take the emotion out of it and base all decisions solely on what's best for the company.

KRISTIN CAVALLARI

VI

You have got to start with the customer experience and work back toward the technology - not the other way around.

STEVE JOBS

Social media is so important to getting the word out there. I think the future of sharing beauty and expertise lies predominantly with the increasing rise of social media.

CHARLOTTE TILBURY

Pursue a career you are passionate about, be prepared to work incredibly hard, and don't sweat the small stuff. Success is an uphill struggle, but hard work pays off in the end.

TAMARA RALPH

Stay positive and keep believing that every problem has a solution.

NOELLA COURSARIS MUSUNKA

Don't let anyone talk you out of your dream and vision Embrace and harness the disruptive changes of the internet and social media which levels the field.

DR BARBARA STURM

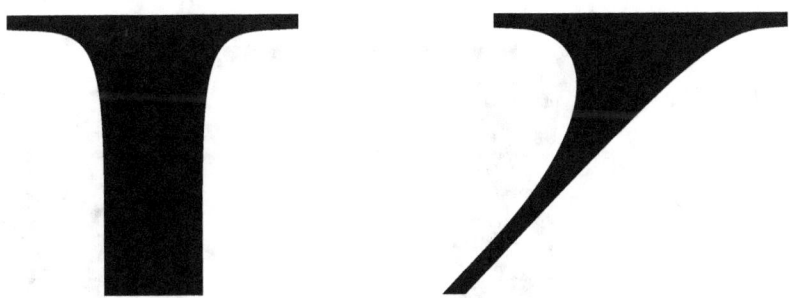

Keep learning and reinventing! Staying in the status quo is death. Cultivate contacts. Build your social media.

ROSANNA SCOTTO

Purpose: Know your why. Business is what we do, but brand is why we do it. You will stray from your why often, but it is imperative that you know it clearly so that you can return to it always.

SAMANTHA WILLS

*Doing the best at this moment puts you
in the best place for the next moment.*

OPRAH

*Find out who you are and be that person.
That's what your soul was put on this earth to be.
Find that truth, live that truth and everything else
will come.*

ELLEN DEGENERES

I

Identify your passion, feed it and commit to it 100%.

EMMA JANE PILKINGTON

D

Don't compare yourself to others. It is a waste of time. That is a setback.

JESSICA SEPEL

Work in an industry that you love.
Don't be afraid to learn from older or younger than you.
Set goals.

PIPPY POMERANZ

If you are successful, it's because somewhere, sometime, someone gave you a life or an idea that started you in the right direction.

MELINDA GATES

Have the courage to follow your heart and intuition

STEVE JOBS

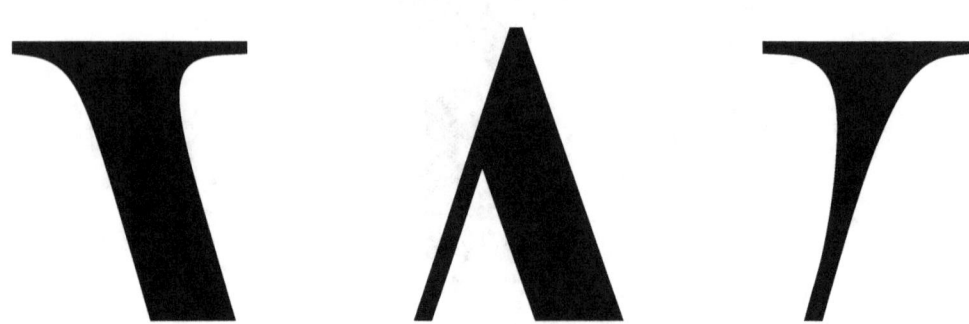

When you are failing, you are forced to be creative, dig deep and think, night and day.

BILL GATES

Y

*Your success, your life, your happiness.
Don't let mean people bring that down.*

TAYLOR SWIFT

*Some women fear the fire,
some actually become it.*

R. H. SIN

You know your on the road to success when you can do your job and not be paid for it.

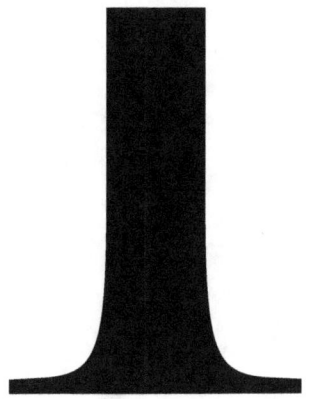

OPRAH

Steph Adams is an accomplished name in the fashion and publishing industry. She is a former model, award-winning digital entrepreneur and #1 best-selling author, who has published ten books.

Completing a Bachelor of Arts degree in marketing, advertising and communications, Steph has worked as an Art Director and over hauled the image of some of the most prestigious magazines from around the world, from Net-a-Porter's very first magazine. She has also lent her eye over other high end publications from British Vogue, Vogue Australia, Harpers Bazaar UK, Marie Claire Australia, Elle UK and Conde Nast Traveler.

Former international model, Steph Adams has been called in for event appearances, appointed an ambassador and fronted social media campaigns for various luxury brands globally.

Over the last decade, Steph has interviewed men and women around the globe making changes, which she has featured in her books; Fashion and Style, Success Secrets, The Game Changers, Citations D'amour, Citations de Bonheur, Beauty and Wellness, Good to Glow and The Juggle.

Steph has been featured across Vogue as "best of front row" and various other magazines as well as news networks and online from, Sky News UK, World News, ABC America, The Daily Mail, Good Morning America, BBC, CNN, Fox Sports, Channel 7's Daily Edition, ABC Radio as well as magazines including; Vogue, Tatler, Glamour Spain, Vanity Fair Italy, Harpers Bazaar, Elle and more.

Steph enjoys supporting philanthropic pursuits and various charities globally.

Instagram: @stephadams2012 www.stephadams.com www.stephadamscreative.com.au

www.ingramcontent.com/pod-product-compliance
Lightning Source LLC
Chambersburg PA
CBHW071121240526
45465CB00022B/750